Dynamic Programming Demystified

Optimizing Code and Mind

Table of Contents

Chapter 1. Introduction

Welcome to this special report, "Dynamic Programming Demystified: Optimizing Code and Mind". In this comprehensive guide, we crack open the esoteric world of dynamic programming and lay it out in the most lucid, digestible format possible. We'll start from the basics, explaining the core concepts in simple, relatable terms before gradually venturing into the practical implementation of this fundamental programming technique. This report is more than just a technical reference; it's an eye-opener that seeks to rewire how you approach problem-solving, optimizing not just your code, but your thought processes as well. It's a journey traversing through the terrains of computer science and cognitive reasoning—a fusion that broadens your horizon as a programmer and critical thinker. Whether you're a coding novice, a seasoned developer seeking to hone your skills, or someone simply interested in learning about the efficiency of dynamic programming, this special report is designed with you in mind. Embark on this thrilling exploration today and unlock new dimensions to your cognitive and coding prowess.

Chapter 2. The Foundations: Understanding the Principles of Dynamic Programming

Dynamic programming (DP), a cornerstone of computer programming, is a technique for optimizing complex problems by breaking them down into simpler subproblems, solving each subproblem just once, storing that solution in a table (usually an array), and using that stored solution so that each solution requires looking up a solution rather than having to compute it again. This might sound like a mouthful, but bear with us – in order to truly understand DP, we will break it down into the following sub-chapters:

2.1. Properties of Dynamic Programming

Dynamic programming principles are primarily applied to problems exhibiting two essential properties: overlapping sub-problems and the optimal substructure.

Overlapping sub-problems refers to a scenario where solving a given problem involves solving the same problem multiple times. In a case without DP, this would lead to an exponential number of redundant operations, causing inefficiencies. But with DP, results from smaller sub-problems (which recur in the solution) are memoized or stored, rather than being recalculated every time.

Optimal substructure property is at play when an optimal solution of a given problem can be obtained by combining optimal solutions of its sub-problems. This property allows us to solve sub-problems once, store these solutions, and construct solutions to bigger problems with the help of the stored solutions.

2.2. Techniques in Dynamic Programming

There are two main techniques of dynamic programming: top-down and bottom-up.

Top-Down (Memoization): This starts with the original problem and breaks it down into its subproblems until reaching a subproblem that is simple enough to solve directly. The solution to each subproblem is stored in a table to avoid duplicating work.

Bottom-Up (Tabulation): The tabulation method starts with the simplest subproblem and iteratively solve larger subproblems until reaching the original problem. This strategy constructs the solution, building up from the base case of the problem.

Both techniques utilize a table to store results of subproblems. However, while memoization fills up the table in an as-needed basis and often in a non-contiguous manner, tabulation fills the table systematically – row by row or column by column.

2.3. Stages of Dynamic Programming

Solving a problem with dynamic programming involves a series of stages:

1. Characterizing a structure of an optimal solution.

2. Defining the value of an optimal solution recursively in terms of smaller sub-problems.

3. Computing the value of an optimal solution in a bottom-up

approach or through memoization (top-down approach).

4. Constructing an optimal solution from computed information.

Let's have a more in-depth look at these stages.

2.4. Characterizing an Optimal Solution

The first step in applying dynamic programming involves defining the structure of an optimal solution. The optimal solution will generally be based on solutions to smaller instances of the same problem. For example, in the shortest path problem, an optimal path to a destination node for a graph can be found by finding the shortest path to the neighboring nodes and then extending the path from there.

2.5. Recursive Definition

Once we've determined the structure of an optimal solution, we can recursively define the value of an optimal solution. In the shortest path problem, the weight of the shortest path would be defined as the minimum weight from the source to a neighbouring node plus the weight of the edge connecting that neighbour. Recursion is the heart of dynamic programming, which breaks a problem into subproblems and constructs the solution from that.

2.6. Computing the Optimal Solution

Computing the optimal solutions to the subproblems is performed in a systematic order. This could either be top-down, where solutions to the subproblems are computed first, or bottom-up, where the simplest subproblems are solved first and these solutions are iteratively used to solve more complex subproblems. The fundamental idea is that since we're using previous computations to find the solution, we don't have to do the same computation again.

2.7. Constructing an Optimal Solution

Finally, once we've computed the optimal solutions for all subproblems, we can determine the optimal solution to the original problem. This usually requires some additional work, because while we've computed the optimal costs or values for the subproblems, we usually need to backtrack through this information to reconstruct what the optimal solution looks like.

This chapter is an introduction to dynamic programming, encapsulating its core principles, techniques, and stages. With these in mind, we will be able to understand practical applications of DP, and how it can drastically optimize our problem-solving ability, resulting in robust and efficient code. Moving on, this guide will outline and explain various problems and how dynamic programming is ingeniously implemented to solve them. Yet, always remember that each problem is unique; a general-purpose solution doesn't exist. Thus, approach these problems with an open, innovating mindset, delving deeper into the beautiful world of dynamic programming.

Chapter 3. Unveiling the Concept: Recursion vs Memoization

In the broad landscape of algorithm design and optimization, two concepts often stand out due to their laudable efficiency and computational prowess: recursion and memoization. Today we shall unravel these key concepts, dexterously unpacking their characteristics, principles, applications, and the crux of their relationship to dynamic programming.

3.1. Understanding Recursion

In computer science, recursion is a method where the solution to a problem depends on smaller instances of the same problem. It involves splitting the problem into subproblems, solving these subproblems, and using the solutions to the subproblems to solve the original problem. Central to recursion are two types of cases: base case(s) and recursive case(s).

Base case(s) represent the simplest form of the problem, a situation that can be solved directly without further recursive calls. On the other hand, recursive case(s) involve a problem that is divided into smaller subproblems solved by recursive calls. Imagine if you have a tower of blocks, and you're tasked with dismantling the tower one block at a time. Taking off each block can be viewed as a recursive call, and reaching the bottom of the tower would signify the base case.

Code for Recursive Factorial Computation

```python
def factorial(n):
```

```
    #base case
    if n == 0 or n == 1:
      return 1
    #recursive case
    return n*factorial(n-1)
  ```
```

Here, the function `factorial(n)` computes factorial of n using a recursive approach. The base case is defined for n = 0 or n = 1. For larger values of n, the function makes a recursive call to compute `factorial(n-1)`, thus applying the very same process to a smaller subproblem.

A major downside to recursion is the concept of overlapping subproblems. They occur when the recursive procedure is called multiple times for the same inputs. This means the same computation is carried out multiple times, forming a significant overhead and rendering the process inefficient especially for larger inputs.

Recursion, though clear and elegant, is not always the most efficient strategy. This brings us to our next essential concept: memoization.

## 3.2. Diving into Memoization

Memoization is a technique for optimizing computing speed by storing the results of expensive function calls, thereby preventing unnecessary computations. The term 'memoization' was introduced by Donald Michie in the 1960s and is derived from the Latin word 'memorandum' meaning 'to be remembered'.

It comes in handy when dealing with overlapping subproblems in recursion. By storing the results of already computed subproblems, we avoid redoing these computations when needed again, thus significantly improving our algorithm's efficiency.
```

```python
def factorial(n, memo = {}):
  #base case
  if n == 0 or n == 1:
    return 1
  #Check the memo dictionary for already computed
factorial
  if n not in memo:
    # compute it and save in memo dictionary
    memo[n] = n*factorial(n-1)
  #return the computed factorial
  return memo[n]
```

Here, the `factorial()` function makes use of an additional `memo` dictionary to keep track of already computed factorials. This way, when a factorial computation is recursive called again, the function checks the `memo` dictionary and directly returns the stored result if it exists, thereby eliminating duplicate computations.

In summary, memoization optimizes recursion by trading off space for time. Essentially, it stores results of potentially recurring computations at the expense of little memory so that subsequent computations can run faster.

3.3. Recursion and Memoization: Synergizing for Dynamic Programming

Having explored recursion and memoization in isolation, it becomes necessary to elaborate on their convergence. As two crucial components of dynamic programming, these concepts must synchronize joyously to ensure operations are performed optimally.

Dynamic programming involves breaking down an original problem into simpler subproblems, solving these subproblems only once, and storing their solutions in case they need to be solved again. In this approach, we embrace both recursion—to break down the problem—and memoization—to store and retrieve solutions efficiently.

They build on each other: recursion ensures problems are broken down into manageable chunks that can be easier solved, while memoization ensures that solutions to these subproblems are readily retrievable when needed. This prevents unnecessary repetitive computations, enhances computational speed, and optimizes memory usage.

Through recursion, we map out the problem space, and through memoization, we remember our journey, all in a bid to make computation an optimal, efficient process.

In conclusion, recursion and memoization are integral techniques fueling the efficacy and efficiency of dynamic programming. They offer a mental model for decomposing and solving problems optimally, a paradigm that extends beyond coding, impacting our broader problem-solving abilities. When harnessed effectively, these concepts could revitalize not only your codebase but also your cognitive toolbox, preparing you to face intricate challenges both within and outside the programming world.

Chapter 4. Conquering Overlapping Subproblems: A Step-by-Step Guide

On first encounter, dynamic programming can appear daunting but at its core, it revolves around simple concepts. Central to understanding dynamic programming is the concept of overlapping subproblems. This chapter aims to elucidate this concept and walk you through a meticulous journey of conquering such problems.

Let's get started by understanding the crux of overlapping subproblems.

4.1. Understanding Overlapping Subproblems

Dynamic programming is generally employed when a problem can be divided into smaller subproblems which are not independent, meaning that they overlap with each other. The solutions of these subproblems are used repeatedly rather than computed afresh each time. Recognizing this property in a problem paves the way for a vastly more efficient solution that takes advantage of these overlaps.

Imagine a scenario where you are travelling through a maze. In the absence of a map, you would be reduced to trial and error, potentially trying the same wrong turn time and again. If, however, you could mark these mistakes (such as dead ends or long loops), then you could avoid repeating them, making your path-finding process markedly more efficient. This is the idea behind solving overlapping subproblems.

4.2. Identifying Overlapping Subproblems

Consider a classic example - calculating the Fibonacci series. The fibonacci sequence follows a simple mathematical relation: `F(n) = F(n-1) + F(n-2)`, with `F(0)` and `F(1)` being 0 and 1 respectively.

If you were to draw a tree diagram, representing the computation of `F(5)`, you'd see that some smaller Fibonacci numbers are computed multiple times. For example `F(2)` is calculated twice while `F(1)` and `F(0)` repeat more often. These are overlapping subproblems.

This overlapping structure signifies that the problem can benefit from dynamic programming.

4.3. A Recursive Approach

The initial instinct to solve such a problem can be to use recursion, innately handling the problem's inherent self-similarity. A recursive function for Fibonacci could be written as follows:

```python
def fib(n):
    if n==0:
        return 0
    elif n==1:
        return 1
    else:
        return fib(n-1) + fib(n-2)
```

Whilst clear and concise, a severe drawback is the repetition of function calls for the same parameters. The larger the value of `n`, the more pronounced this inefficiency becomes.

4.4. Memoization: A Vital Tool

This is where we introduce our first tool for dynamic programming: memoization.

Memoization is a technique in which you store the results of expensive function calls and reuse them when the same inputs occur again. In terms of our Fibonacci function, once we compute F(2), for instance, we store the result somewhere. If F(2) comes up again in our computations, we simply look up the stored result instead of calculating it afresh. This makes our problem solving process significantly faster.

The `fib` function, when adopting memoization, might look something like this:

```python
def fib(n, memo):
    if memo[n] is not None:
        return memo[n]
    if n==0 or n==1:
        return n
    else:
        result = fib(n-1, memo) + fib(n-2, memo)
        memo[n] = result
        return result

def fib_memo(n):
    memo = [None] * (n+1)
    return fib(n, memo)
```

In this function, `memo` is an array to store calculated values. Our Fibonacci function now checks if we've computed a result for a given input n before. If so, we return that result. If not, we compute it, store it in `memo`, and then return it.

4.5. Bottom-up Approach

Another strategy besides memoization is the "bottom-up" approach, directly building the solution iteratively. In our Fibonacci problem, we begin computing from the smallest subproblems $F(0)$ and $F(1)$, gradually working our way up to the desired solution, in this case $F(n)$.

The "bottom-up" Fibonacci function could be represented like so:

```python
def fib_bottom_up(n):
    if n==0 or n==1:
        return n
    fib = [None] * (n+1)
    fib[0] = 0
    fib[1] = 1
    for i in range(2, n+1):
        fib[i] = fib[i-1] + fib[i-2]
    return fib[n]
```

This method effectively eliminates the requirement to keep track of "already computed" problems (as in memoization), since we naturally avoid solving a subproblem more than once by dynamically programming the calculation in an orderly fashion.

4.6. Cracking your own Problems

Having understood overlapping subproblems via the example of the Fibonacci sequence and investigated approaches to conquer them, you can apply these strategies to your unique scenarios.

Given a problem, start by determining if it can be broken into overlapping subproblems. Test out a recursive solution and observe if there are multiple calculations for the same parameter. If so, congratulations, it's a good candidate for dynamic programming!

Try implementing the memoization technique for a recursive solution, then attempt a bottom-up approach, constructing the solution from smaller problems. Experimenting with both helps gain a practical understanding of dynamic programming.

Finally, do not forget that mastering dynamic programming is a journey. It's akin to complex puzzle solving, it requires diligent effort, continual practice, and a keen sense of observation to get better. Most importantly, it's vital to remember your successes as you start to unlock the potential of dynamic programming.

With these in-depth insights into overlapping subproblems, we have the basis to delve deeper into dynamic programming. We are now equipped to explore further concepts and optimization methods, to write efficient codes that seamlessly handle complex problems. It is not just an enhancement of computational capacity, but instills a profound logical acuity, reshaping our thinking and problem-solving approach in this digital era.

Keep on exploring, practicing, and coding!

Chapter 5. Getting Practical: Simple Examples to Dive Into

Now that we have acquainted ourselves with the theoretical aspects of dynamic programming, it's time to apply these concepts to practical examples. Remember, we learn best through practice. We'll start with simple examples and gradually move to more complex scenarios. Rest assured, by the end of this chapter, you'll feel more confident in applying dynamic programming techniques.

5.1. Understanding the Sub-problem Structure

The ability to identify a sub-problem structure is key to implementing dynamic programming. In most dynamic programming problems, the larger problem can be divided into smaller, overlapping sub-problems.

Let's consider the classic example: The Fibonacci series. It is a sequence where each number is the sum of two preceding ones. Can you spot the sub-problem? If we were computing the 5th Fibonacci number, we would need the 3rd and 4th Fibonacci numbers, which in turn would require the 1st, 2nd, and 3rd numbers, and so on. This repetitive structure of sub-problems is the first indication that a problem is suitable for a dynamic programming solution.

Here is a simple top-down recursive algorithm written in Python to calculate the 'n'th Fibonacci number:

```python
def fib(n):
    if n <= 1:
        return n
    else:
```

```
    return(fib(n-1) + fib(n-2))
```

Notice the repeated calculations? Many recursive solutions suffer from this issue of recomputation.

5.2. Caching to the Rescue: Memoization

Memoization is a technique to store the results of expensive function calls and reuse them when the same inputs occur again. This is done to avoid recomputing the same result, thereby optimizing our code.

Let's use memoization in our Fibonacci series example:

```
def fib(n, memo={}):
    if n <= 1:
        return n
    elif n not in memo:
        memo[n] = fib(n - 1, memo) + fib(n - 2, memo)
    return memo[n]
```

Now, our function remembers the results of previous calculations and reuses them when necessary. This dramatically reduces the function calls needed and speeds up our code.

5.3. From Top-Down to Bottom-Up: Tabulation

Formally, the tabulation technique is the opposite of the top-down approach and mainly involves filling a table (usually an array or a matrix) in a bottom-up way. The table structure helps in storing intermediate results of sub-problems.

Here's how we can write the Fibonacci series algorithm via tabulation:

```python
def fib(n):
    fib_table = [0, 1] + [0] * (n - 1)
    for i in range(2, n + 1):
        fib_table[i] = fib_table[i - 1] + fib_table[i -
2]
    return fib_table[n]
```

We first create a table of 'n' elements, all initialized at 0, except the first two elements set to be the first two Fibonacci numbers, 0 and 1. We then fill up the table from left to right. Each new entry is just the sum of the two preceding entries.

5.4. Exploring More Cases: The Coin Change Problem

Next, let's consider another classic dynamic programming problem known as the Coin Change problem. The problem states: "Given an amount and the denominations of coins available, determine how many ways change can be made for the amount, using these coins."

Here's the solution using tabulation:

```python
def coinChange(coins, amount):
    dp = [0] + [amount + 1] * amount
    for coin in coins:
        for x in range(coin, amount + 1):
            dp[x] = min(dp[x], dp[x - coin] + 1)
    return dp[amount] if dp[amount] != amount + 1 else
-1
```

The function first prepares a dynamic programming table, dp, which stores the minimum number of coins needed to make change for different amounts. The function iterates over each coin, and for each coin, it updates the dp table for all amounts larger than or equal to the coin value.

This chapter should provide a good starting point for your exploration of dynamic programming. By practicing these examples and trying to apply the dynamic programming approach to new problems, you can further enhance your understanding and proficiency in this area.

Chapter 6. Mastering the Art of Decision-Making: The Optimal Substructure

Dynamic programming is built upon a principle called "Optimal Substructure". Recognizing that a problem has an optimal substructure is the key to uncovering the potential for using dynamic programming. It is fundamental to every problem that we can solve with dynamic programming, and the first step on the journey to mastering the art of decision-making.

An optimal substructure is a property of a problem whereby an optimal solution can be constructed from the optimal solutions of its smaller, overlapping sub-problems. Determining whether a problem has an optimal substructure traditionally involves dividing the problem into smaller pieces, solving each piece independently, and finally, consolidating the smaller solutions to form a global solution. But within the realm of dynamic programming, we approach this differently. We exploit this characteristic by solving each smaller sub-problem only once and storing the result, which reduces computing time significantly.

6.1. The Concept of Optimal Substructures

Optimal substructure is, at its core, a way to define a problem in terms of simpler versions of itself. It often goes hand in hand with another fundamental dynamic programming concept: "overlapping subproblems". While overlapping subproblems relate to the instances when a single subproblem appears multiple times, optimal substructure refers to the fact that the global optimum can be determined by the optimum solution of its subproblems.

Take the classic example of computing Fibonacci numbers. The Fibonacci sequence is a series of numbers where a number is found by adding up the two numbers before it. So, to find the nth Fibonacci number, you first need to find the (n-1)th and (n-2)th numbers. Notice that both of these calculations also need the previous two numbers, and so forth. So, the problem of finding the nth Fibonacci number is broken down into two smaller, simpler problems. This is the optimal substructure at work.

6.2. Recognizing Optimal Substructures

The most striking sign of optimal substructure is when a problem involves making multiple choices and the correct decision cannot be made without solving one or more similar smaller problems. For instance, in pathfinding or shortest path problems, to find the shortest path from point A to B, we must find the shortest path to each of the points along the way. These, in turn, involve finding the shortest path to yet other points. If we can define the problem in terms of these smaller steps, we have an optimal substructure.

In dynamic programming, recognition of an optimal substructure often comes into play when solving problems related to number theory, graph theory, combinatorics, game theory, probability, string/data array processing, and much more. It is important to thoroughly define the problem and understand its properties before reaching a conclusion about the presence of an optimal substructure.

6.3. Utilizing Optimal Substructures

There are two primary techniques for utilizing optimal substructures: top-down (memoization) and bottom-up (tabulation). Both these approaches exploit the optimal substructure in different ways.

Top-down is simply a perspective shift from the conventional divide-and-conquer approach, where we solve the problem in its regular sequence, using memory to remember the outcome of each subproblem. This approach is known as "memoization".

On the other hand, the bottom-up approach, or "tabulation", starts with the simplest subproblem and iteratively computes each one, saving the results in a table, until reaching the final subproblem.

While both of these approaches accomplish the same goal, your choice between the two should be decided by the specific requirements and constraints of the problem you're trying to solve.

6.4. Training Your Brain for Optimal Substructure Recognition

Becoming proficient in recognizing optimal substructures requires ongoing practice with a variety of problems. However, several strategies can accelerate your progress.

First, understand the problem thoroughly. Being able to determine the underlying mathematical or structural properties of a problem will lead you towards recognizing its optimal substructure.

Second, break the problem down into smaller components. If it can be defined as a combination of smaller instances of the same problem, it might have an optimal substructure.

Lastly, look for repeat computations. If computed results are being utilized repeatedly, you've another indication of the presence of an optimal substructure.

By incorporating these strategies into your problem-solving process, you will improve your abilities in not just programming, but effective decision-making as well.

In conclusion, the concept of optimal substructures is a crucial part of dynamic programming. Understanding and utilizing this concept can greatly help in making your code faster, more efficient, and ultimately, more dynamic. Remember, the key to dynamic programming lies not just in the mechanics of coding, but chiefly in the efficient decision-making and problem-solving techniques. Start recognizing the patterns, understand the overlaps, and exploit the grand puzzle of optimal substructures.

Chapter 7. The Power of Tabulation and Bottom-Up Approach

Dynamic programming harnesses the power of tabulation and a bottom-up approach to yield optimized solutions for complex problems. It's an algorithmic strategy rooted in breaking down the larger problem into subproblems, computing and storing their solutions, ultimately building to solve the overarching problem. The bottom-up method begins from the simplest subproblems, gradually advancing towards the more complex ones.

7.1. Understanding Tabulation

Tabulation is an approach wherein we solve a problem by creating a table and filling it in a bottom-up, iterative manner. The tabulation technique usually involves building up an n-dimensional table to hold the answers to subproblems. Here, 'n' refers to the number of parameters that can change the answer to our problem. Once we've computed the table, we can find the solution to our initial problem by observing the final few entries in the table.

For an illustrative example, let's take the Fibonacci sequence. If we consider a conventional recursive method of computing the nth Fibonacci number, we would compute the (n-1)th and (n-2)th Fibonacci numbers as subproblems. However, with tabulation, we start from the foundation: the 0th and 1st Fibonacci numbers. Then, we iteratively calculate the next Fibonacci numbers until we reach 'n', keeping all the interim results in a table. This process effectively avoids the redundant recalculations encased in the plain recursive method.

```
|===
| Fibonacci Numbers | 0| 1 | 1 | 2 | 3 | 5 | 8 |  list
continues...
| Index | 0| 1 | 2 | 3 | 4 | 5 | 6 |  list continues...
|===
```

You'll find that the overall time complexity is much lower compared
to the top-down approach as we've eradicated the redundancy.

7.2. The Advantages of Tabulation

Understanding the upside of any approach gives us the enthralling
Why behind its usage. Tabulation, manifesting itself in dynamic
programming, provides several concrete benefits.

1. Tabulation eliminates the need for recursion and, thereby,
   reduces the need for a call stack. A larger stack size could
   potentially lead to a Stack Overflow error. As such, tabulation is
   effective for problems with larger input sizes.

2. Tabulation involves iteratively solving subproblems, which
   indicates that it's guaranteed to cover all the subproblems. No
   subproblem will be ignored or missed.

3. Due to the bottom-up approach, there's no re-computation of
   subproblems. We calculate each subproblem exactly once and
   store its result, thus enhancing efficiency.

4. Tabulating results in a table provides an intuitive, visual way of
   observing how the solution progresses. This representation aids
   in problem comprehension and debugging.

7.3. Defining The Bottom-Up Approach

The bottom-up approach, closely linked with tabulation, refers to an algorithmic practice starting from the base cases (smallest, simplest subproblems) and iteratively building the solutions for larger and more complex subproblems. This approach embraces the spirit of "Solve locally, think globally".

To contrast, the top-down or recursive approach begins with the larger problem and breaks it down into smaller subproblems. In dynamic programming, this could lead to repeated computation of some subproblems.

7.4. The Bottom-Up Approach in Action

Imagine you're tasked to compute the factorial of a number 'n'. The conventional method would be to employ recursion, multiplying 'n' with the factorial of 'n-1'. With the bottom-up approach, you start from the base case, i.e., the factorial of 0, and build your way up to 'n'. This simplifies the algorithm, removes the dependency on recursion and boosts performance.

```
|===
| Factorial of Numbers | 1 | 1 | 2 | 6 | 24 | 120 | 720
| list continues...
| Numbers | 0 | 1 | 2 | 3 | 4 | 5 | 6 | list
continues...
|===
```

This modification may seem minor when dealing with a low-stakes computation like factorials, but in larger problems, this change in approach can transform an algorithm from infeasible to optimal.

7.5. The Power of the Bottom-Up Approach

Harnessed correctly, the bottom-up approach brings a gamut of advantages, including:

1. Reduced time complexity through avoidance of repeated subproblem resolution.

2. Lower space complexity as there's no need to maintain a stack trace, unlike in recursive solutions. This directly implies that this approach is ideal for larger input sizes.

3. Solutions to all related subproblems are available and stored systematically, aiding in debugging and overall understanding of the problem's landscape.

4. The deterministic nature of this approach guarantees the generation of an optimal solution.

7.6. Conclusion

The tabulation technique and bottom-up approach form the essence of dynamic programming. By segmentifying the problem into manageable subproblems, storing and reusing their results, we can improve the efficiency and readability of our code. This paradigm not only brings ease to you as a coder but also efficiency to the machine by reducing time complexity. The visual representation and systematic approach for solution-finding help in understanding a problem more intuitively—from its base case to complex versions. This methodology ultimately optimizes not only the performance but also your strategy as a problem solver. So the next time you're faced with a complex problem, think tabular, think local but aim global - that's the essence of dynamic programming.

Remember, every large problem is simply a collection of smaller problems waiting to be solved. Through the astute usage of tabulation and a bottom-up approach, you're better equipped to solve any problem—be it in your code or your cognitive space.

Chapter 8. Advanced Techniques: Tackling Complex Real-World Problems

We begin this exploration by delving into the utilization of dynamic programming to tackle complex, real-world problems. As we proceed, the intricacies of developing algorithms and deriving high-performing solutions will unravel.

8.1. Understanding Problem Complexity

Real-world problems are complex, often involving multiple variables, constraints, dependencies, and non-obvious choices. A classic introductory problem in dynamic programming is the knapsack problem, where the goal is to choose items with maximum value, given a fixed total weight capacity. However, real-world problems are much more convoluted and multifaceted. Dynamic programming provides an optimal framework to tackle such issues, enabling us to break them down into smaller subproblems, solving each once, and then collating the results to derive a comprehensive solution.

8.2. Formulating Problem Statement

An integral part of dynamic programming is to accurately represent a complex problem concisely. Once we have the problem statement, we need to identify what the inputs and outputs are. For instance, while working on a scheduling software for employees, the inputs might be employee availability, task durations and deadlines, and the output could be the optimized schedule reducing idle time and maximizing timely task completion. The problem statement also necessitates recognizing the constraints, which, in this case, could be the maximum and minimum hours an employee is allowed to work.

8.3. Breaking Down into Subproblems

The magic of dynamic programming truly shines when we disassemble a large daunting problem into manageable subproblems. However, it's crucial to identify how these subproblems interrelate. We are looking to discern any overlapping, i.e., repeated computations, and then pursue a mix of top-down (memoization) and bottom-up (tabulation) approaches to store and recall these values and reduce computational redundancy.

For example, consider a problem where we are trying to minimize the cost of cutting a piece of rod into smaller pieces. The various subproblems could be the costs associated with cutting the rod to different lengths.

8.4. Finding a Recursive Solution

Once the subproblems are identified, developers often find a recursive algorithm to manage them. For many, this moves against their intuition to find a direct, often iterative, solution. The crux of dynamic programming is this ability to find a recursive structure in a problem, providing a clear path to solve it more efficiently. Let's think about Fibonacci numbers; to find the nth Fibonacci number, one needs the (n-1)th and (n-2)th numbers. This requirement is straight-up recursive.

8.5. Memoization and Tabulation

Memoization and tabulation are techniques pivotal to optimizing recursive algorithms. Memoization refers to maintaining a 'memo' or records of computed results for specific inputs, allowing one to reuse this data rather than re-computing. This system is the essence of the top-down dynamic programming approach.

On the other hand, in the process of tabulation, we solve all related subproblems in a fixed order, which ensures that before solving a problem, all of its dependent subproblems have been solved already. This technique is a part of the bottom-up dynamic programming approach.

8.6. Pseudo-polynomial Time Complexity and NP-Complete Problems

Many real-world problems fall under the category of NP-Complete problems, such as the Travelling Salesman Problem or the Subset Sum Problem. Dynamic programming provides pseudo-polynomial time algorithms for these, wherein the time complexity is polynomial in the numerical value of the input but exponential in the length of the input.

8.7. Conclusion

Dynamic programming is an extraordinarily powerful technique, but it comes with its challenges. Formulating the problem statement, identifying subproblems, defining recursive relations, and ensuring optimal time complexity are steps that require a deep understanding of the problem at hand and a sound grasp of algorithmic thinking.

Our journey has equipped us with knowledge about the effective deployment of this methodology, but like all things, it demands practice. We must continue refining these skills, utilising them in increasingly intricate real-world problems, constantly learning, and growing as computational thinkers and problem solvers.

Next, we will envelope ourselves in a deeper dive into the nuances of dealing with dynamic programming problems, providing an artefact of wisdom to further our growth in this field.

Chapter 9. Cognitive Angle: The Mindset Behind Dynamic Programming

To demystify dynamic programming, it's necessary not only to comprehend the abstraction of its algorithms but also to grasp its essence within the framework of a programmer's mindset. In this chapter, we attempt to explore how our cognitive approach affects the implementation of dynamic programming and how the application of these strategies can transform our thought processes.

9.1. Understanding the Paradigm

Dynamic programming (DP) is as much a mindset as it is a coding technique. It revolves around a 'bottom-up' approach to solving problems where the initial simple problem forms the basis for gradually expanding and solving more complex problems. This demonstrably contrasts with the 'top-down' reasoning which we frequently employ to tackle problems in our daily lives, where we typically look at the broader picture and then attempt to connect the dots. However, in DP, we start connecting the dots (solving smaller sub-problems) before the broader picture (the overall problem) even materializes.

This approach requires the ability to dissect a complex problem into simpler sub-problems, and the discipline to solve these sub-problems systematically, storing their solutions for future reference. This approach is not only efficient but also implements the core principle of DP – overlapping sub-problems. By realizing that the same sub-problems are being repeated, we can save these results and reuse them to eliminate redundancy and save computational time.

9.2. The Beauty of Dynamic Programming

The allure of Dynamic Programming lies in its elegance and efficiency. It offers a structured path to reach solutions, fostering an organized mindset that considers the fundamental relationship between sub-problems and the overall problem. It discourages haphazard and inefficient approaches to problem-solving, coercing programmers to think about optimizing their code for both space and time complexity.

For those new to DP, it's important to remember that it is not a magic wand that can be waved over all types of programming problems. Rather, it's a tool specifically designed to address problems that exhibit two key characteristics: optimal substructure and overlapping sub-problems. A problem demonstrates optimal substructure if its optimal solution can be constructed from the optimal solutions of its sub-problems. Overlapping sub-problems are present if a problem can be broken down into sub-problems which are reused several times.

By learning to recognize these characteristics in a problem, you not only master DP but also strengthen your analytical skills—learning to scrutinize a problem and understand its nature before hastily rushing into code. This cultivated patience and focus are invaluable assets in the vast toolkit of a successful programmer.

9.3. The Matrix of Problem Solving

In dynamic programming, we often approach problems with the concept of tabulation. This involves creating a matrix or table to systematically store and reference the results of sub-problems. The visual and structured nature of a tabulation aids in clarifying the links between sub-problems and their parent problem. Additionally, this provides programmers with a clear trail of thought, helping them visualize DP's stepwise, cumulative approach to reaching a solution. Often, the tabulation process also reveals patterns within the problem that can guide further optimization of the solution.

In addition to enhancing your problem-solving abilities, creating such matrices enables the development of visualization skills that are essential in algorithm design and debugging. It instills a rigorous yet creative mindset that can apply multi-dimensional thinking to problem-solving, a skill pertinent not only to DP and computer science but also to broader realms of logical reasoning and thinking.

9.4. Pacing the Learning Curve

Despite its benefits and allure, dynamic programming has a fame for being daunting to beginners due to its perceived complexity and the shifts in mindset it necessitates. One key aspect to understand is that mastery in DP (like most areas of programming and computer science) doesn't happen overnight. It requires patience, perseverance, and above all, practice.

Each problem you encounter refines your decomposition skills, revealing new facets of patterns and techniques embedded within dynamic programming. As you improve, you'll find that you're not only becoming more adept at DP, but you're also improving as a coder in general. The skills you gain from learning DP—logical reasoning, problem dissection, and optimization—are transferable to many other aspects of programming.

9.5. Final Thoughts

In essence, dynamic programming isn't just about writing efficient code; it's about adopting a mindset that values careful problem-decomposition, patient execution of tasks, and meticulous optimization of solutions. Though potentially intimidating at first glance, a slow and steady journey into this field promises invaluable lessons that transcend the realm of coding, extending into life's diverse problems. The cognitive approach behind dynamic programming is just as integral, if not more so, as the code itself, underscoring the synergy between the mental and technical realms that define successful programming.

Conquering dynamic programming demands more than just technical prowess—it requires a mindset shift, a willingness to embrace new ways of thinking, and the ability to reimagine the way we approach problem-solving. It's an expedition of discovery, where the ups and downs we encounter help sculpt our cognitive and coding skills, making us adept problem solvers in an increasingly complex world.

Chapter 10. Building Efficiency: Tips and Tricks for Optimization

Efficiency stands as a cornerstone in the world of programming. It defines how quickly a program executes, how much memory it consumes, and how effectively it can scale. Optimizing your project thus boils down to increasing its efficiency—making judicious use of resources such as time and space, while also engineering an appropriately fast and flexible solution. Inside of this chapter, we'll delve into the heart of such optimization processes, unveiling some of the quintessential tips and tricks for enhancing the efficiency of computer programs in the context of dynamic programming.

10.1. The Art of Memoization

Memoization, a key technique underpinning dynamic programming, leverages the concept of "remembering" previously performed computations to expedite future calculations. The rationale here is simple: why repeat a task you've already done? If you have a function performing a certain calculation more than once, you can store the results of these calculations in a data structure (like an array or a hash table), and then directly fetch these results the next time the same calculation is needed, hence shunning any redundant computations.

To illustrate, consider the famous problem of finding the nth Fibonacci number. In a naive recursive implementation, the computation of the same subproblems is repeated multiple times. This leads to an exponential time complexity. However, by using memoization, you store the result of each subproblem and reuse it when the same computation occurs again. This reduces the time complexity to linear.

Implementing memoization often involves three simple steps:

- Initialize a cache (an array or a dictionary) to store the computed results.

- In your function's code, before making the computation, check whether the result for the current input is already available in the cache.

- If it's there, return it. If not, perform the calculation, store the result in the cache, and then return the result.

10.2. Top-Down vs Bottom-Up Approach

Dynamic programming solutions can be broadly categorized into two styles: the top-down approach and the bottom-up approach.

In the top-down approach, also known as memoization or the method of deferred decisions, you start solving the problem by breaking it down. If you see that the problem has been solved already, then just return the saved answer. If it has not been solved, solve it and save the answer. This is usually easy to think of and very intuitive.

On the other hand, in the bottom-up approach, you solve all the sub-problems first (hence the "bottom"), and then combine their solutions to reach an answer for the main problem. This is particularly useful when the problem asks for the count of ways, or the optimal way to do something, as opposed to asking for a Boolean value, like whether something is possible.

In the context of dynamic programming, the choice between a bottom-up and top-down approach depends largely on the problem at hand. Some problems might lend themselves to a simpler solution using top-down recursion with memoization, others may be more efficiently addressed using a bottom-up approach, circumventing recursion entirely.

10.3. Choice of Data Structures

Data structures are another crucial element for optimizing dynamic programming solutions. The choice of the right data structure can significantly speed up your program. Often, for dynamic programming, the choice is between one- or multi-dimensional arrays.

Using a one-dimensional array can be a good fit when the current state of the problem depends only on the immediately preceding state. An example of such a problem would be finding the nth Fibonacci number, where the nth Fibonacci number depends only on the (n-1)th and (n-2)th Fibonacci numbers.

However, if the current state of the problem depends on several previous states, you might want to consider using a multi-dimensional array. Take, for instance, the 0/1 Knapsack problem. In this problem, the current state (i.e., the maximum value that can be achieved with a given weight) depends on multiple previous states. Thus, a two-dimensional array will be a good fit here.

10.4. Exploiting Overlapping Subproblems

One of the key principles that make dynamic programming effective is its ability to exploit overlapping subproblems. Overlapping subproblems refer to subproblems that recur many times in the process of solving the main problem. Recognizing these overlapping subproblems is often the first step to designing an efficient dynamic programming solution.

Suppose you're trying to compute the shortest path from a start point to an end point in a given graph. In this case, the problem of computing the shortest path between two points can be broken down into smaller subproblems, such as finding the shortest path to intermediate nodes. If these subproblems are solved independently, there will be many redundant calculations.

By identifying and optimally handling these overlapping subproblems, you can significantly reduce computation time. In this problem context, you could opt to store the shortest computed distances in a cache. Then, when computing subsequent distances, you would first check the cache to avoid recalculating the same distances over and over.

10.5. Debugging Dynamic Programming Solutions

Debugging dynamic programming solutions can be challenging, mainly due to the recursive nature of many such solutions. However, there are a couple of effective tricks to simplify the debugging effort:

1. Whenever you write a dynamic programming solution, especially if you are implementing a complex decision-making routine, ensure to thoroughly go through the logic in your head and on paper before you start coding. This can help prevent many bugs from creeping into your code in the first place.

2. Use print statements or a debugger to examine the content of your memoization table or array. This can be extremely helpful in uncovering any issues with the memoization process.

3. Run your solution with a base case or a simple case that you can solve manually. Compare the output of each step with your manual results to see if it conforms with your expectations.

4. If you are using recursion, think hard about your base case and ensure it is correctly formed. Most problems in highly recursive dynamic programming solutions come from an incorrect base

case.

In conclusion, building efficient dynamic programming solutions is a multi-step process. It requires a strong understanding of the problem domain, the ability to break down problems into subproblems, appropriate usage of memoization, tailoring your approach (top-down or bottom-up) to fit the problem, choosing the right data structures, rightly exploiting overlapping subproblems, and utilizing effective debugging strategies. With these tips and tricks, you are on your way to unpacking optimized solutions for complex problems. The mantra is: think, code, debug, optimize, and repeat. Happy coding!

Chapter 11. Bridging Code and Mind: The True Power of Dynamic Programming

Dynamic programming enables a significant leap towards highly efficient problem-solving. By breaking problems down, reusing solutions of smaller sub-problems, it optimizes both the execution of code and the thought processes behind problem-solving strategies. Embracing dynamic programming equals to establishing an intimate connection between how you think and how you code.

11.1. The Conceptual Bridge: Grasping Dynamic Programming

Before diving into a storm of complex codes and problem sets, we first lay the groundwork - studying the conceptual essence of dynamic programming. At its core, dynamic programming operates on two key principles: Optimal Substructure and Overlapping Subproblems.

The principle of optimal substructure regards that solutions of a problem depend on solutions to smaller instances of the same problem. Figuring out a way to the peak of a mountain, for example, requires knowing the best route to a halfway point.

Conversely, overlapping subproblems occur when a recursive algorithm could solve multiple identical subproblems. Contemplating a game of chess, we often analyze numerous sub-games within the broader context, many of which, ironically, have the exact outcomes.

Dynamic programming draws on these principles to optimize computation, storing solutions of subproblems so they don't have to be recomputed time and again.

11.2. Unfurling the Mystique: Dynamic Programming in Action

The real magic starts when dynamic programming breathes life into lines of codes. Let's utilize a classic problem: the Fibonacci Sequence. A naive recursive approach would be CPU-intensive due to repeated calculations. With dynamic programming, it transforms into an ingeniously simple, linear operation, storing previously computed results in an array to avoid re-computation.

With dynamic programming, no extra effort is required as each calculation is performed only once, thereby saving both time and computational power. The process brings to light the innate connection between code optimization and efficient problem solving.

11.3. Mind Over Code: Cognitive Benefits of Dynamic Programming

Dynamic programming does much more than boosting codes - it optimizes cognitive abilities. As a programmer, adopting a dynamic programming approach prompts strategic thinking, enhances problem-solving skills, and shapes a detail-oriented mindset. Write code that tackles Fibonnaci sequence with dynamic programming, you're not merely writing a piece of software; you're improving your logical and analytical thinking.

Applying dynamic programming principles leads to disjointing complex problems into manageable units, tackling them effectively, understanding their interconnections, and storing the solutions for future reference. It manifests a model of organized thought and strategic problem-solving, valuable in programming and beyond.

11.4. Framework to Function: Mastering Dynamic Programming in Practice

Moving from abstract concepts to concrete applications, we encounter the real power of dynamic programming through practice. It could be as simple as optimizing recursive codes for computing factorial numbers or as complex as solving the knapsack problem, which finds extensive applications in resource allocation and decision-making.

Applying dynamic programming to these situations, we initially define a simple recursive solution. Next, identify overlapping subproblems and optimize using dynamic programming—Store results of each subproblem, reusing them later. Iterative or bottom-up solutions, from the simplest subproblem to the complex ones, help bridge understanding and code implementation.

11.5. Conclusion: The Unseen Path of Dynamic Programming

Dynamic programming is not merely an algorithmic concept; it is a way of thinking, a strategic problem-solving approach that transcends the realm of code to enhance cognitive abilities. It connects the mind's abstract problem-solving strategies and the computer's concrete executions of code - a bridge between thought and action, idea and implementation.

It is empowering, enabling you to tackle complex computational problems with ease and practicality. So, embrace dynamic programming. Understand its principles, apply them in practice, and witness how it can transform not only your code but your thought processes. Embrace this powerful technique that truly exemplifies the convergence of code and mind. Transform your understanding of problem-solving, imbibe the spirit of strategic and organized thinking, and evolve, as dynamic problem solvers of the future.